HOW TO WEAR
JEWELLERY

———

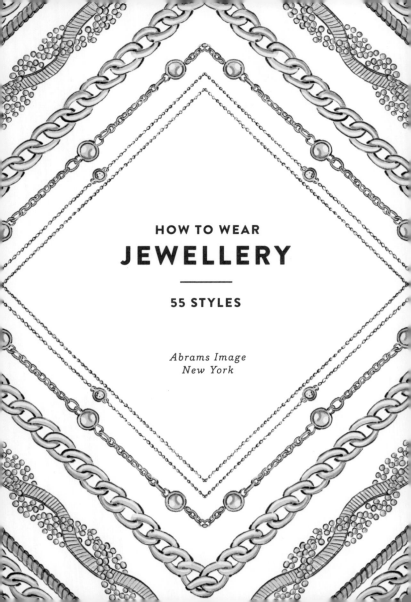

HOW TO WEAR
JEWELLERY

---

55 STYLES

Abrams Image
New York

Table of
CONTENTS

INTRODUCTION
6

INTRODUCTION

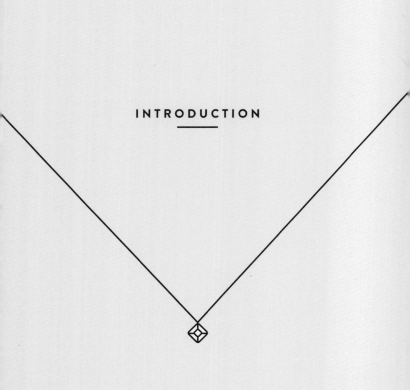

Throughout the ages, jewellery has served as symbolic totems and as a creative outlet to embellish appearance. From ancient Egyptian amulets believed to ward off evil to the infamous ropes of pearls favoured by Coco Chanel, the function and style of jewellery has evolved, but its glittering presence has remained steadfast.

HOW TO WEAR JEWELLERY presents a range of styles for everyone—opulent costume show-stoppers; whimsical, barely there pieces; traditional pieces set in classic materials—and offers inventive ways to wear necklaces, bracelets, earrings, brooches, rings, and more. Whether you're a seasoned bauble hoarder or a novice ready to kick-start a collection, consider this a guide to inspire your *bijoux* for years to come.

CHAPTER
ONE

SIGNATURE STYLES

Icons + Inspiration

SIMPLY CLASSIC

E legant pearls, tasteful diamond touches, and a few well-chosen pieces for the wrist—classic jewellery never goes out of style. It's no wonder single strands of pearls and sets of diamond earrings have been coveted standby items for generations; they quickly elevate and refine any look.

SIGNATURE PIECES

PEARL NECKLACES // DIAMOND STUDS // PEARL BROOCHES // GOLD BANGLES AND CUFFS // TENNIS BRACELETS // CHARM BRACELETS // SIGNET RINGS

More is more and nothing is off-limits—including sparkling bracelets, stacks of large geometric rings, clusters of heirloom pins, and maxed-out chunky necklaces. But don't mistake the magpie approach for lowbrow or lazy—every costume piece is carefully selected, and when worn together, the combination transforms into an artful work worthy of appreciation.

SIGNATURE PIECES

COCKTAIL RINGS // LARGE COLLAR NECKLACES // OVERSIZED BROOCHES // MULTI-STRAND NECKLACES WITH SEMI-PRECIOUS STONES // STACKABLE BANGLES

ARTFULLY MINDED

Geometric pendants, abstract drop earrings, angular rings—these are the jewellery pieces that could be considered modern art in their own rights. It's these bold pieces that add the final touch to a black-on-black ensemble or bring additional depth to a colourful outfit. When the pieces are carefully selected, the artfully minded jewellery wearer becomes a bona fide curator.

SIGNATURE PIECES

GEOMETRIC PENDANTS AND RINGS // SQUARE BANGLES // ABSTRACT PINS // MARBLE MOTIFS // CUBIC-CUT GEMSTONES

UPDATED HEIRLOOM

Aged rings that bear engraved monograms, gemstone pieces that have been passed down for generations, breathtaking antique finds that have been unearthed at flea markets—these priceless heritage pieces are full of character. Whether your heirloom jewellery is worn on its own or incorporated in with modern pieces, nothing makes an outfit more timeless than antiques.

SIGNATURE PIECES

ANTIQUE RINGS AND NECKLACES // MOURNING JEWELLERY // GEMSTONES (onyx, moonstone, and turquoise) // GOLD LOCKETS // VINTAGE BROOCHES

DIY CHIC

Necklaces strung with homemade beads, friendship bracelets woven with care, and custom rings soldered in small studios—the best kinds of jewellery are the ones that are handcrafted with love by the jewellers who designed them. With the resurgence of DIY jewellery and one-of-a-kind designs available in stores and online, these artisanal accessories might just become the new classics.

SIGNATURE PIECES

WOVEN NECKLACES AND BRACELETS // CAST-METAL EARRINGS // WOODEN BANGLES AND BROOCHES // GLASS- AND CLAY-BEAD NECKLACES // FRIENDSHIP BRACELETS

MODERN BOHEMIAN

The modern bohemian invokes whimsy through an eclectic mix of jewellery that is as free-spirited as it is chic. Playfully combining a range of global influences—from a touch of brightly coloured turquoise or a dappling of oxidised silver to yards of multicolour beaded necklaces—these pieces create a perfect picture of a stylish bohemian.

SIGNATURE PIECES

WESTERN AND TRIBAL MOTIFS // TURQUOISE AND BEADED NECKLACES // LEATHER AND SILVER CUFFS // CRYSTAL PENDANTS // HEADBANDS

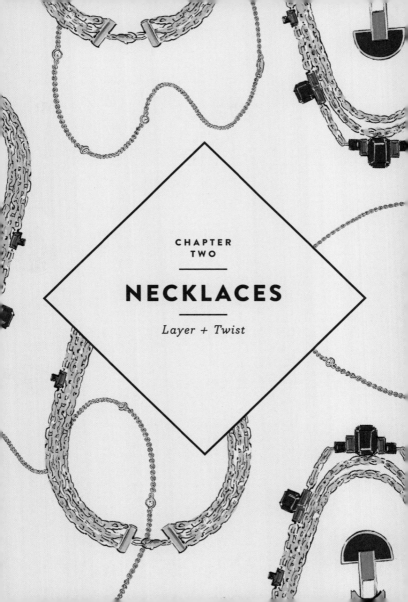

CHAPTER
TWO

NECKLACES

Layer + Twist

Necklaces are true finishing pieces.
A colourful statement necklace adds
character and interest to simple outfits;
considered gold chains and ropes of
pearls imbue elegance; multi-layered
strands of beads, box chains, and
pendants hint to personality and taste.

Here are the most common necklace styles to know:

CHAIN — a long series of metal links that serves as a foundation for necklaces and can be worn solo or with a pendant

PEARL — a string of incandescent beads, derived from pearl oysters and molluscs, that comes in a variety of lengths

CHOKER — a simple necklace—usually made from leather, fabric, or thin metal—that fits snugly around the middle of the neck

PENDANT — an ornamental charm that hangs from a necklace

BIB — a decorative bib-shaped necklace that fits at the collar, usually held together by a series of looped chains

COLLAR — a necklace that fits at the collar of the neck and imitates the neckline of a button-down shirt

STATEMENT — an extravagantly stunning necklace full of colourful pieces or stones that draws attention

MULTI-STRAND — a necklace with more than one strand of pearls or chains attached to the clasp

In the pages ahead, you'll rethink how to style pearls, learn a foolproof way to layer dainty necklaces, see what necklines work best with your pieces, and more.

14"

16"

18"

20"

24"

30"

33"

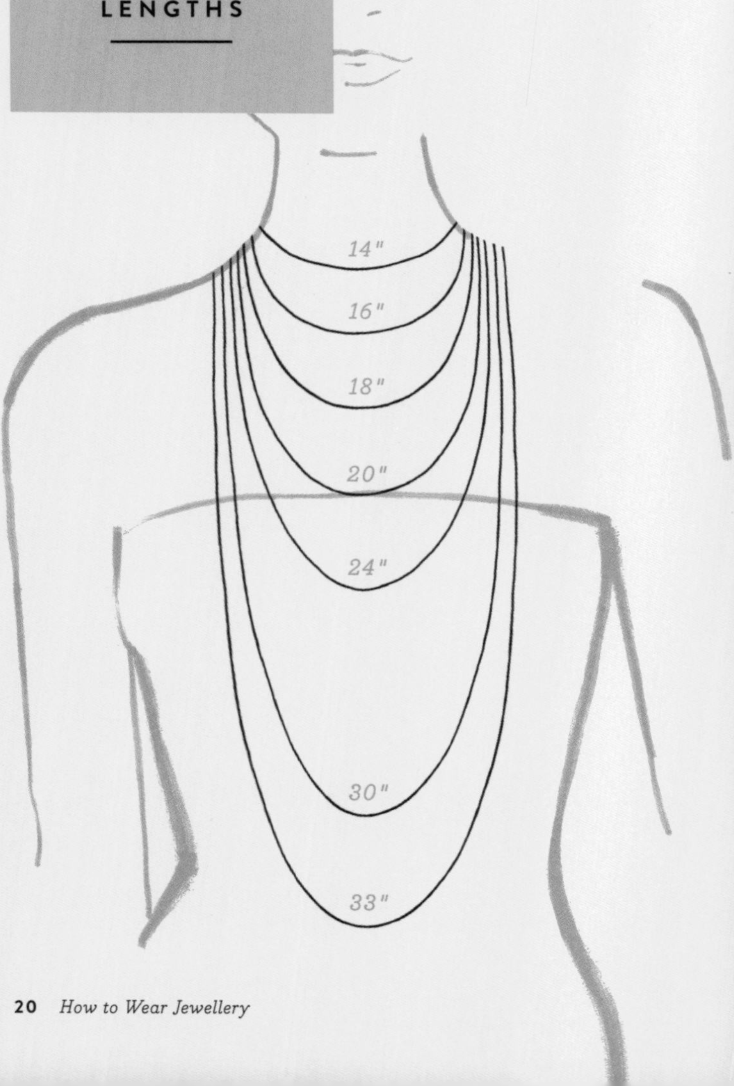

Whether you're choosing a necklace for a night out or building a multi-layered look, these measurements are a simple guide to making it all work.

14" (35.5 CM) CHOKER

Choker necklaces fit snugly around the middle of your neck.

16" (40.5 CM) COLLAR

Collar necklaces sit comfortably at the base of your neck, where, as you've guessed, most collars on button-downs finish. Bib necklaces are most associated with the collar length.

18" (46 CM) PRINCESS

The princess necklace gets a bit more breathing room and drops down to the upper-chest area. You'll find plenty of statement necklaces and pendants dangling at this chain length.

20-24" (51-61 CM) MATINEE

The matinee necklace generally hits mid-chest, and, as the name suggests, leans towards a casual afternoon look. Beaded necklaces and longer pendants tend to fall in this area.

30" (76 CM) OPERA

The opera necklace scoops below the breast and pairs nicely with more formal frocks. Chains and long strands of pearls end at these plunging lengths.

33" (84 CM) ROPE OR LARIAT

The super-long rope necklace is the most dramatic—it hangs near the waist. Vintage necklaces that you can slip on and loop twice around your neck are generally found at this stunning length.

How to
LAYER

DELICATE CHAINS

1

Start with the most delicate piece. Wear the lightest, most-delicate necklace closest to the neck, following with heavier necklaces as you layer.

2

Space out the necklaces. Make sure each piece has breathing room. While the spacing of each necklace doesn't have to follow exact measurements, be mindful that they don't lie on top of one another. Note how the second bar necklace is about a half-inch (12 mm) from the first necklace, but the third necklace hangs an inch (2.5 cm) from the second.

3

Mix metals and textures. Box chains, gold bars, beaded necklaces, and small stones— layer different metals and styles as you go. Note how the beaded necklace second from the bottom adds texture to a look that is mostly made up of chains.

4

Anchor the entire look with your largest pendant. The heaviest pendant and longest chain necklace should always sit at the bottom layer to help anchor the entire look. If you try to layer another necklace below a pendant, the spacing between the necklaces will look unbalanced.

Delicate chains are pretty enough to wear on their own but so much more fun to layer with other dainty necklaces. Once you know the rules of how to pile them on, you can layer your chains in a million ways.

MATERIALLY MAXED OUT

1

Select one centrepiece. Start with your most prominent statement piece as the base. The centrepiece has a bit more weight than the others—it's the one showcased in the middle. Here, the base piece is the stunner that hangs second from the top. See how that one piece does a lot of the heavy lifting? Without it, the look wouldn't be as robust.

2

Layer around the centrepiece. Next, select two additional bold necklaces—one that falls just above the base necklace and one that falls just below it—and layer them on. There will be inevitable overlapping, so just be sure that the necklaces aren't directly on top of one another. (You wouldn't want a collision of those precious stones and that vintage beading!)

3

Add a few easy chains. To finish the look, throw on one or two simple chains of varying lengths to add depth to this massive neck party. Look into wheat chains or box chains—they tend to work best because of their hefty shapes and textures.

AUTUMN ▶

An edgy statement necklace is the perfect piece to wear with a soft, silken collared shirt to create nice textural contrast for autumn. Wear your statement piece closer to the neck to accentuate the bib-like quality of the necklace.

◀ WINTER

Choose pieces that are big enough to compete with a winter coat, and wear them around chunky-knit roll necks to complement the weight of your outfits.

Despite its bravado, the statement necklace is easily adaptable year-round. Take a look at how these bold numbers can work through the changing seasons.

SPRING ▶

It's all about florals in the springtime, so pair a jewelled statement bib with a bright shift dress to add an extra punch of colour and shine. To liven up a casual look, wear the necklace with a simple white T-shirt.

◀ SUMMER

To celebrate the shining summer sun, opt for a statement necklace with electric brights. Limit yourself to wearing just one showpiece (to stay cool), and pair the necklace with a seasonally appropriate strapless top.

ROLL NECK ▶

Pair a longer necklace with a roll neck to help elongate your torso.

◀ CREW NECK

A bib necklace works best when it's worn exactly like a bib—over a simple, clean-cut crew neck to play up the effect of a secondary collar.

STRAPLESS ▶

A necklace that peacocks all the way around needs to be seen from every angle, ideal for a strapless look.

If you've ever questioned which necklines work best with your necklaces (or ever wondered which would best show off a beloved piece), let this visual cheat sheet be your foolproof guide.

SQUARE NECK ▶

If you've got a square or boxy pendant to flaunt, showcase it with a corresponding square neckline to match the geometric shape of the charm.

◀ SCOOP NECK

Pair a decorative, U-shaped necklace with a similarly rounded scoop neck—the neckline won't impede the ornate pendants.

BOATNECK

For an unexpected way to showcase long, beaded necklaces, wear them over a wide boatneck revealing a hint of shoulder.

How to Wear
PEARLS

KNOTTED

Knotting your jewellery is
normally not encouraged,
but with a long strand of pearls,
it's an easy way to transform
a simple necklace.

HOW TO STYLE

If you're keen on wearing
a menswear-inspired trouser
suit, pearls bring a touch of
femininity. Keep them knotted
to maintain a streamlined look.

Pearls, as lovely and timeless as they are, can sometimes get a bad rap for being too formal. So we're twisting up these long ivory gems for a new take on the classic.

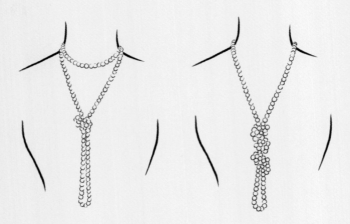

// VARIATIONS //

1 Loop a long strand of pearls twice around your neck. Adjust the two strands so the bottom loop sits matinee length (approximately 20 inches / 50 cm). Tie a knot in the bottom loop to create a "loosened-tie" look.

2 If a single knot isn't doing it for you, give your strand multiple knots to create larger pearl clusters. You can either keep knotting over the same one knot for a snowball effect or knot in succession for a more uniform approach.

PINNED

Nothing elevates a set of pearls more than adding an ornate pin or brooch. Opt for a decently sized pin in a complementing metal or decorated with non-clashing semi-precious stones.

HOW TO STYLE

Embellish a ladylike look by adding a pinned pearl necklace. The pearl-and-gemstone combination is an easy way to bring more detail to a simple dress.

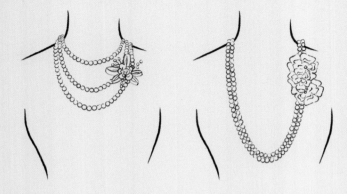

// VARIATIONS //

1 *Loop your pearls so they sit in three lengths and pin a flowery brooch with gemstones or pearls directly onto your jumper to keep the desired length in place.*

2 *Loop your pearls twice to have the double strands sit at opera length and use a single floral brooch to pin them together. Attach the pin near the chest area, where you'd normally pin a brooch.*

TWISTED

Give your strands a modern update with a super-messy twist that will make you look mighty put-together.

HOW TO STYLE

Liven up a blazer/jumper combo with a set of twisted pearls. For additional texture, layer these pearls with a gemstone necklace under a shirt collar—the satin finish of pearls contrasts nicely with the sparkle of gems.

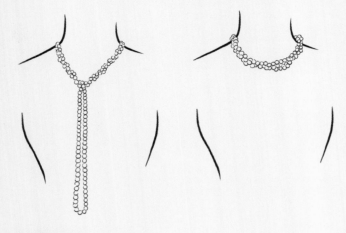

// VARIATIONS //

1 You'll recognise the basic
pull-through—a common
scarf-tying move that involves
pulling one end of the necklace
through the loop of the other
end. To add much-needed
interest and movement, simply
twist a choker-like set of pearls
a few times.

2 Fold a long strand of pearls
in half and twist the ends around
in opposite directions until it
shortens to fit comfortably
around the base of your neck.
Wrap the twisted set of pearls
and use a small brooch or pin
as a clasp to attach the two ends
together at the back of the neck.

How to Wear a
REVERSE
NECKLACE
—

The backwards necklace, the reverse necklace, the backdrop— no matter what you call it, this dramatic turn-it-around style was a favourite of Coco Chanel, who wore her ropes of pearls backwards. Remember, the whole point is to show off these back skimmers, so pull your hair forwards or into a fine up-do.

LARGE PENDANT ▶
- -
Keep it ultra-simple with two or three medium-sized pieces. Select one short necklace and one long necklace, with about two inches separating them, and play around with varying pendant shapes and chain textures.

GEMSTONES ▲

Turn a lavish bib necklace
around for a black-tie look.
A simple scoop-back dress
works well for a shorter
statement necklace.

DELICATE CHAINS ▶

Select a beautiful Y-necklace
made with thin chains. Pair this
necklace with a dress with an
exposed back that plunges as
far as the necklace drops.

BROOCHES

Pin + Cluster

Brooches and pins are the hardest-
working pieces of jewellery. These
bijoux are not only beautiful
embellishments, but also markers of
clubs and societies, historical bearers of
lineage, and functional pieces that hold
garments together with style.

Here are the most common brooches and pins to know:

STICK PIN—a small, delicate, lollipop-like brooch attached with a longer stick pin

CAMEO—an intricate carving, usually of a woman's profile, traditionally carved from a semi-precious gemstone such as onyx or agate

ANNULAR—a piece circular in shape that has the pin running across the diameter of the brooch

HAIR—a brooch that incorporates the hair of a passed love one into the design, also know as mourning jewellery

VINTAGE—a pin that originates from a previous era

LAPEL PIN—a small enamel pin usually worn on the lapel of a jacket or other outerwear to represent membership to an organization

In this chapter, we take a gander at the inventive ways your brooch collection can enhance a garment, breathe new life into accessories, and end up in unexpected places.

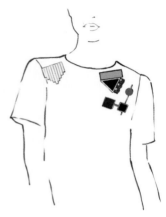

VINTAGE GOLD
- -
If you're looking to class up
your office attire in a jiffy, select
any number of vintage gold
brooches—look for tiger's
eye stones, pearls, gems, and
sunburst stick pins—and attach
them to the lapel of a blazer for
an easy upgrade.

GEOMETRIC
- -
If your neutral outfit is in need
of a little boost, opt for pins
that feature strong geometric
shapes, asymmetry, or expert
colour-blocking.

Whether you stick to vintage semi-precious stones or prefer colourful floral pins, there's a brooch out there for everyone.

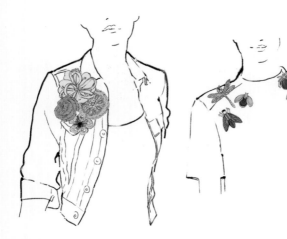

FLORAL

Make it a garden party and pin several flowery brooches onto a light jacket. To keep floral pins from looking precious, attach them to a tougher fabric such as denim to keep things casual.

INSECTS

Nobody wants a bug crawling around on their shoulders, but bejewelled critters are another story. For a real conversation starter, pin a few gorgeous bug brooches on a clean slate such as a white top.

If you've got 'em, flaunt 'em. For a powerful punch, pin on an overload of brooches, concentrated on the shoulders and chest.

1

Wear a sturdy blazer jacket. Choose a jacket with thick fabric—like heavy tweed, corduroy, or denim—that will support the weight of the brooches.

2

Mix and match metals. To keep the brooches looking cohesive, stick to similar-looking metals such as all silver, brass, or gold, or a mix of complementing metals that are matte or shiny.

3

Work around the anchor pieces. When creating the maxed-out brooch look, start with your two largest statement brooches and pin each of them to a different side of the blazer. These will serve as the anchors.

4

Surround the anchored pieces with smaller pins. Space out the medium-sized brooches on both sides of the blazer and fill in any gaps with smaller pins as finishing pieces.

5

Create symmetry. To find a balanced look, aim to form as much symmetry as possible on both sides of the blazer. This means dividing equal amounts of medium- and small-sized pieces on both sides.

6

Max it out. Select a range of materials: diamond brooches, pearl pins, modern designs, vintage motifs, and a variety of gemstone colours that complement the overall theme.

How to Wear
COLLAR PINS+
CHAINS

_____

POINTED
COLLAR PINS ▶
- -
For subtle embellishment,
attach collar pins—one on
each collar tip—to bedazzle
a dress shirt. Keep necklaces
to a minimum to make these
pins really stand out.

◀ MAXED-OUT
CHAIN BROOCHES
- -
An elegant way to dress
up a blouse is to attach a
maxed-out chain brooch—
multiple chains, ornamental
pins—for ultimate collar flair.

Jazzing up the collar of your button-down has never been so easy. Button your shirt all the way up and attach these collar pins for a simple upgrade.

JEWELLED COLLAR PINS ▶

If you don't have pointed collar pins, select two similar lapel pins or smaller brooches that can still attach to the collar. Diamond or silver brooches look stunning on silk shirts.

◀ SIMPLE CHAIN BROOCHES

Make a crisp white Oxford more interesting with a simple chain brooch. The embellishment looks particularly on point if you're wearing the top tucked into black trousers.

SPRING ▶

Get out your enamel floral brooches and line them up around the neckline of your favourite dress to create an eclectic and colourful arrangement.

◀ AUTUMN

There's nothing like a bejewelled vintage brooch to add that touch of personalisation to an autumn jumper. Position your brooch directly under your collar for a snug fit.

Here's how to make brooches work with your outfits every season. Whether you're bundled up or removing layers, brooches can add a much-needed accent to any ensemble.

WINTER ▶

Go big and bold with two matching oversized brooches on a collared coat. Heavy-duty brooches work best for this look since delicate brooches risk getting broken.

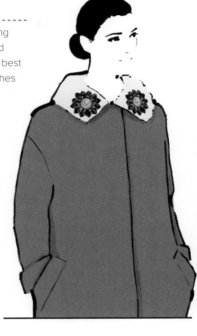

◀ SUMMER

Keep it simple for summer—if you're wearing a collared shirt, adorn the collar tips with a chain brooch.

Since single brooches tend to look lonesome on a top or a jumper, pair one with a necklace to take your outfit to the next level.

BIG GEMS

Pair a vintage gem brooch with a statement necklace to boost the sparkle factor. Rather than wearing the brooch on your chest, attach it between the points of your blouse collar like a bow. The symmetry of the brooch with a jewelled bib necklace looks particularly polished.

OLD-SCHOOL CHARM

If you're looking to find a necklace
companion for your classic pin of
gold, pearls, and black leather,
match it with chunky strands of
gold chain links. This combo works
well because the chains in the
necklaces match the link shape
and colour of the pin.

DELICATE LAYERS

A delicate pin like the one shown
above—an arrow with a thin
decorative chain hanging from
it—is pretty on its own, but its
daintiness can get lost easily on
a jumper. Pair a smaller pin with a
tiered necklace, as these pieces
will simultaneously complement
and enhance each other.

Put a Pin
ON IT

ON YOUR LOAFERS ▶

Grab a set of small insect pins
and attach them to your shoes
for fancy feet. Fabric loafers
make excellent candidates since
they tend to hold pins far better
than other shoe materials, such
as leather. Plus, you can remove
the pins at the end of the day
and your shoes won't be ruined.

◀ ON YOUR SCARF

Add some fun to your
chunky knit scarf by
attaching a large vintage
brooch to it (the pin can
also work to keep your
scarf in place). Keep the
brooch pinned to the side
to achieve a subtle touch of
embellishment.

*It's as easy as it sounds! Discover ways to easily embellish your
other accessories just by pinning them creatively.*

ON YOUR HAT ▶

Accentuate your hat with a
quirky pin—it adds character to
what would otherwise be just
another basic accessory. This
works all year round, too: You
can pin a floral brooch to a straw
hat or attach a vintage gemstone
brooch to a winter hat.

▲ IN YOUR HAIR

You can attach barrettes, bobby pins, or a hair comb
to a brooch to secure it in your hair. Another tactic
involves pinning a brooch to a long piece of ribbon
that can then be used as a headband.

CHAPTER
FOUR

BRACELETS

Pile + Clasp

Bracelets are versatile pieces of jewellery that can play more than a supporting role dependent on style. Large artful cuffs, Fifth Avenue enamel, plastic bangles, and delicate gold links can be worn solo, stacked unexpectedly, or doubled on each wrist for maximum effect—there are limitless ways to re-imagine the bracelet.

Here are the most common bracelet styles to know:

CUFF—a wide split metal bracelet that fits right over the wrist

BANGLE—a usually non-flexible hoop bracelet to be slipped over the entire hand

CHAIN—a linked-metal bracelet of a variety of styles, including box, figaro, snake, wheat, and rope shapes

CHARM—a chain bracelet with very large links from which charms and trinkets hang

DIAMOND—a fine metal bracelet with individually set diamonds that go all the way around (also known as a tennis bracelet)

FRIENDSHIP—a DIY bracelet made from a series of colourfully knotted threads or strands of yarn

Read on for the low-down on how to master the ultimate bracelet stack, how to style bracelets for the changing seasons, and the best way to build around a simple leather band. Whether you're looking for a way to adorn your naked wrist or you're in the mood to switch up your everyday arm look, you're sure to find a bracelet style that stacks up to your taste.

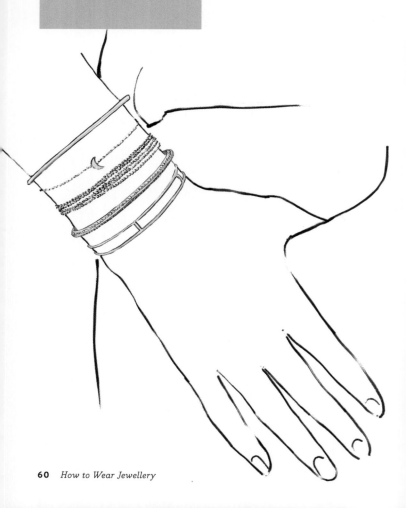

Stacking bangles, chains, straps, charms, and cuffs is a simple way to mix up your collection. Whether you prefer a delicate look or want to pile on the statement pieces, use the style breakdown below to help update your bracelet game.

THE DELICATE STACK

1

Start with delicates. Select similar bracelets—thin chains, bangles, and cuffs—that fit snugly around your wrist. Bracelets that are too thick overcrowd the wrist and add weight.

2

Mix bracelet styles and textures. Note how each of these bracelets is slightly different. Selecting a variety of styles—chains, bangles, diamonds—helps diversify the look.

3

Space them out according to fit. It's best to dress up your wrist based on how the bracelets fit. Bangles are non-adjustable and tend to be on the bigger side, so keep them higher on the arm, whereas daintier, adjustable bracelets can rest closer to the hand.

4

Go easy on diamonds. The key to any delicate stack is subtlety and proportion—limit yourself to one super-sparkly bangle if the other stackables are low-key.

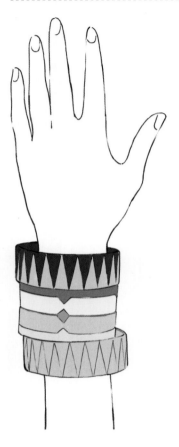

◄ **THE ENAMEL STACK**

Select your bangles. Select up to three styles similar in width, design, and palette to keep the look cohesive.

Double the fun. Stack up the other arm with similar-looking enamel pieces to create a symmetrical look.

Wear an outfit that complements the stack. Enamel bracelets can be worn casually or more formally, so whether you're wearing a T-shirt or LBD, opt for shorter sleeves to let the bracelets shine.

THE FRIENDSHIP STACK ▶

Choose friendship bracelets turned luxe. Look for pieces that embody the DIY spirit with sophisticated materials such as colourful silk cords, gold beads, and tassels.

Stack them silly. When it comes to mixing multiple friendship bracelets, nothing beats a carefree spirit. Pile on the pieces and let them overlap.

Wear an outfit that complements the stack. Wear these colourful bracelets with a vintage T-shirt and a denim jacket with the sleeves rolled.

◀ THE PATTERNED-BANGLE STACK

Wild out on patterns. When it comes to printed plastic bangles, select the boldest styles to mix and match while staying in the same colour scheme.

Alternate thick and thin. Stack so that thick bangles are interspersed with thinner ones. Notice how the two widest bangles are spaced well apart to retain proportion.

Wear an outfit that complements the stack. Choose a low-key, solid-colour dress to showcase the stack or go bold on a similarly patterned-out ensemble.

THE SOUTHWESTERN STACK ▶

- -

Select your silvers. The vibe of the Southwestern stack is simple: turquoise, silver, and Native American–inspired motifs. The silver here isn't highly polished, so choose toned-down finishes such as nickel and oxidised silver.

Stack them strategically. Wear the bracelets as they fit best on the wrist, alternating wide and thin bracelets.

Wear an outfit that complements the stack. Since the Southwestern stack is pretty fine-tuned to the bohemian look, this stack tends to look best with flowing, floral dresses or fringed leather vests.

How to Work in a
WATCH

Beginning with a key timepiece, here are the staples you need in your arsenal to create limitless combinations.

1

Start with a watch. Depending on your personal style, select a versatile watch made with materials that will easily lend themselves to your everyday wear. Common watch options include leather or plastic straps, metal or jewelled links, a large or small face, and analogue or electronic functionalities.

2

Add an interesting cuff. The cuff may be simple in shape but they can come in many intricate designs. Even if it's your only bracelet, you can always count on a cuff to make your arm look a bit more finished and to complement your watch.

3

Choose a delicate chain or two. Small gold chains rest easily on top of a watch. They're subtle enough for everyday wear and beautifully simple.

4

Throw in a bangle. The one-size fit means there are no pesky clasps to deal with, so it's a must-have piece for watch-stacking purposes.

WINTER ▶

- -

To accessorise with winter
wear, select a wide, luxe
bangle cuff or two to stack
over a sleek leather glove
for the cold weather.

◀ **SPRING**

- -

Choose a single sculptural
metal cuff with cut-out details
to match the breeziness of a
spring outfit.

Even as temperatures rise and fall, there are always opportunities to wear your bracelets.

SUMMER ▶

Summer is all about keeping things light and colourful, so layer delicate beaded bracelets with bright friendship bracelets (or other pieces that won't get too sweaty on your wrist).

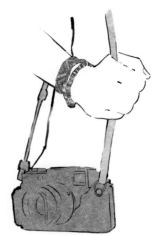

◀ AUTUMN

Layer on pieces with oversized gold links, rich leather straps, and lush accented textures like tortoiseshell and wood to reflect autumn's earthy tones.

Two Ways to Wear
GOLD CUFFS

———

Versatility is key when it comes to investing in a piece of jewellery. Here are two different ways to wear the standard gold cuff bracelet—one for the office-going weekday and the other for the off-duty weekend.

WEEKDAY

- -

For a touch of office bling, wear your gold cuffs over the sleeves of your Oxford button-down. Go ahead and roll up the sleeves of your power blazer, too.

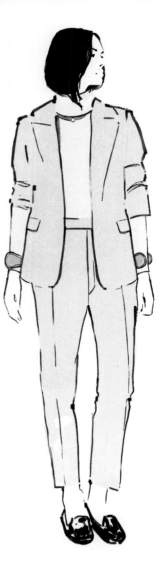

WEEKEND

For a casual afternoon look, slip your gold cuffs over the sleeves of an oversized boyfriend shirt and top off the easy look with a denim jacket.

Three Ways to Wear
LEATHER
BANDS
_____

Most people associate leather bands with the straps of their watches. Fair enough; it's the everyday utility of the material that makes leather essential. It's softer than plastic and lighter than metal, and it has a crafty vibe to it. Check out how you can incorporate leather into your everyday stack.

◄ THE SIMPLE STACK
- -
Choose a few thin leather bands to stack on top of one another.

ADD CHAINS ▶

Mix gold and leather to create
a deluxe saddle look. Since
leather appears a bit more sturdy
and heavy-duty, match your
metals accordingly and go for
oversized gold chain links.

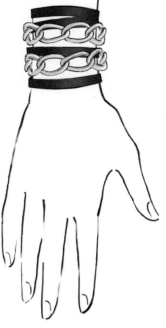

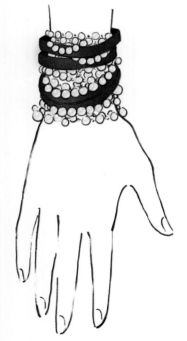

◀ ADD PEARLS

An eclectic way to dress up a
leather bracelet or tone down
a strand of pearls is to take one
of each and wrap them into one
harmonious blend.

CHAPTER
FIVE

RINGS

Stack + Curate

Ornamental and symbolic, these small pieces can hold significant meaning. From engagement show-stoppers to traditional signets, rings are often the most personal pieces of any jewellery collection.

Here are the most common ring styles to know:

ENGAGEMENT—a ring, usually set with a diamond or gemstone, that represents engagement for marriage

WEDDING BAND—a ring that is worn after a wedding ceremony to denote marital status

SOLITAIRE—a ring that bears a single gemstone on a plain band

FIDELITY (OR PROMISE)—a ring that signifies relationship status and usually depicts interlocking hands or a knot

ETERNITY RING—a ring that has individually set stones around the band

COCKTAIL (OR COSTUME)—an opulent ring, with one oversized gemstone or semi-precious stone, often made with affordable materials

ANTIQUE—a vintage ring that dates back to an earlier era

FIRST-KNUCKLE RING—a small ring that fits in between the first and second knuckles

SIGNET—a personalised ring bearing an emblem, crest, or initials

CLASS—a ring to signify a membership to a society, group, or institution

Learn how to proportion your delicate rings, see how to do the costume stack in a non-clunky way, discover how to actually wear first-knuckle rings, and more. Get your fingers ready for some glitz and glamour—these looks are ringing with style.

Knowing your ring size will come in handy if you're seeking a custom piece, looking to resize an existing ring, or ordering a ring online and cannot try it on in person.

To find your ring size, wrap a piece of string or a thin strip of paper around your finger and mark it. Every finger is shaped differently, so measure the finger on the hand where you intend to wear a particular ring.

Measure your finger's circumference in millimetres and match it to the corresponding ring size shown opposite. If your measurement falls in between numbers, it's recommended you size up. (This sizing method works for first-knuckle rings as well.)

For best results, measure your finger towards the end of the day, when your hands are naturally larger from the day's activities.

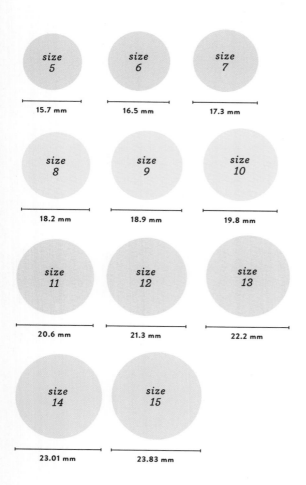

size
5

15.7 mm

size
6

16.5 mm

size
7

17.3 mm

size
8

18.2 mm

size
9

18.9 mm

size
10

19.8 mm

size
11

20.6 mm

size
12

21.3 mm

size
13

22.2 mm

size
14

23.01 mm

size
15

23.83 mm

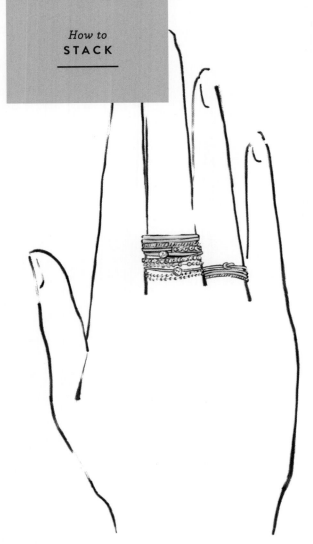

Even though rings are relatively small, they can have a big impact on any look. Make them loud and proud with an assortment of costume pieces or lean towards subtle and sweet with an arrangement of thin gold bands. Here's how to stack them up.

THE DELICATE STACK

1

Select your stackables. The key to any great delicate ring stack is texture and variety. Small chain rings, beaded wire rings, square wire rings, round wire rings, and small gem rings can all work in harmony to create the perfect power stack.

2

Mix them up. Once you have your collection of rings, it's time to get building. While there's no hard rule about the order of rings, it's best to space out different styles. For example, note how the gem and beaded rings are interspersed between the simpler bands.

3

Stack between the knuckles. The height of the ring stack depends on how short or long your fingers are. If you're going for a power stack (as seen on the middle finger), stay within the knuckles so that your fingers can actually move around. If you've got shorter fingers, this means your stack may consist of fewer rings.

4

Play with proportion on other fingers. If you have one power stack, keep the other fingers more low-key with two or three rings per finger.

1

Select an assortment of statement rings. This includes costume pieces, precious gems, mixed metals, and interesting bands of varying widths. Commit to this curated hodgepodge look and go bold.

2

Pick one ring to be the showpiece on each hand. It's ideal to wear the largest statement ring on the middle finger so that the other rings can be styled around it. The showpiece on the right hand is the massive vintage three-stone ring. (On the left, it's the double stone on the ring finger.) Keep the right proportions by dressing around these rings with smaller pieces.

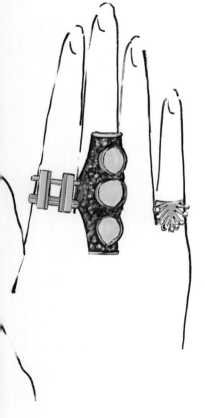

Double the fun. You don't have to utilise every finger (the unadorned fingers are just as important for balance), but use both hands for a maxed-out look.

1

Select your first-knuckle rings.
First-knuckle rings, also known
as midi rings, are the small rings
that fit between the first and
second knuckles of a finger. Most
first-knuckle rings are dainty,
perfect for wearing with other
delicate rings.

2

Look for variety. While first-
knuckle styles are normally
thin, you can still find rings with
various shapes to mix and
match. Look for double-stacked
rings, cut-outs, and textured
bands that have hammered or
twisted metal.

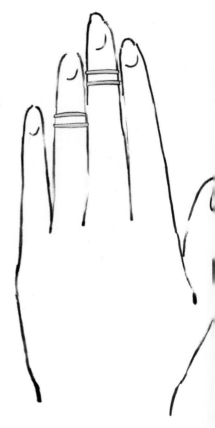

3

Utilise all knuckles (not just the first knuckle). You can wear a first-knuckle ring solo, but it looks even better with a regular ring stack. Play around with alternating knuckles on different fingers.

4

Keep proportions in mind. As with any jewellery stack, be mindful of balance. If you're already stacking several rings on one finger, you will probably want to lighten things up on the next finger, stack a bit more on the next one, and so on. Just don't overload—keeping a few fingers naked makes this look that much more artful.

GEOMETRY
OF RINGS

Consider these three easy geometric solutions to take the guessing game out of keeping rings proportional.

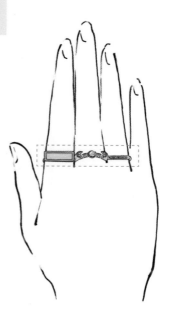

IN A STRAIGHT LINE

Wear three rings of the same width in a straight line—across your index, middle, and ring fingers. It's easy ring styling at its best.

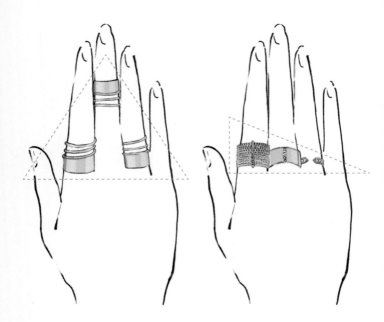

IN A PERFECT TRIANGLE
- -
Select two rings, one for your
index finger and one for your
ring finger. Complete the trinity
with a midi ring around the first
knuckle of your middle finger,
and voilà—a perfect triangle.

IN A RIGHT TRIANGLE
- -
Create a right triangle by wearing
your thinnest ring on your ring
finger, followed by a slightly
wider ring on your middle finger,
and finishing it off with your
widest ring on your index finger.

ARTFULLY MINDED ▶

Pair angular rings with a spherical precious stone to round things out.

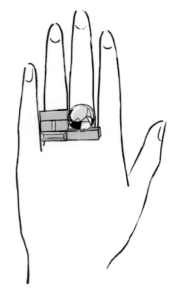

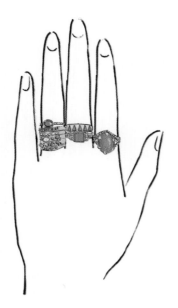

◀ CURATED GEMSTONE

Thin bands, Art Deco pieces, cocktail rings—as long as the gemstones are consistent, these rings will complement one another.

SIMPLY CLASSIC ▶

Nothing says classic like
a stack of diamonds with
a signet ring for a touch of
personalisation.

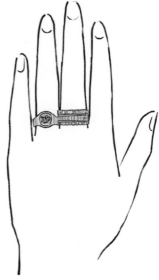

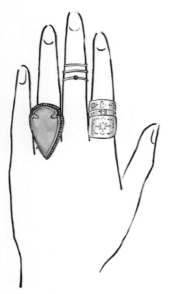

◀ MODERN BOHEMIAN

Go for bold ring cuffs with
Southwestern-inspired
designs to bring the whole
bohemian vibe together.

Marquise	*Round*	*Trilliant*
This almond-shaped diamond cut has the largest surface area for facets.	The round diamond cut is the most popular and classic style—it was the first standardised cut due to its brilliancy and reflection of light.	This diamond cut refers to all triangular-shaped diamonds and can either have straight or curved edges.
Oval	*Pear*	*Square*
The oval diamond cut creates the illusion of a large surface area and can elongate the finger.	A hybrid of the round and marquise diamond, the pear cut usually displays excellent craftsmanship due to its symmetry.	A square-shaped diamond with step cuts means that the facets are more broad and flat, making the stone less brilliant than a stone with more facets.

Identify the common cuts of your favourite gemstones with this handy cheat sheet.

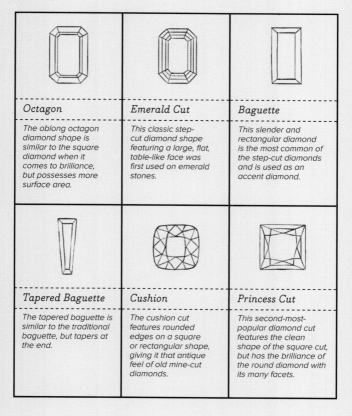

Octagon	**Emerald Cut**	**Baguette**
The oblong octagon diamond shape is similar to the square diamond when it comes to brilliance, but possesses more surface area.	This classic step-cut diamond shape featuring a large, flat, table-like face was first used on emerald stones.	This slender and rectangular diamond is the most common of the step-cut diamonds and is used as an accent diamond.
Tapered Baguette	**Cushion**	**Princess Cut**
The tapered baguette is similar to the traditional baguette, but tapers at the end.	The cushion cut features rounded edges on a square or rectangular shape, giving it that antique feel of old mine-cut diamonds.	This second-most-populer diamond cut features the clean shape of the square cut, but has the brilliance of the round diamond with its many facets.

CHAPTER
SIX

EARRINGS

Cuff + Pierce

Earrings are totems of tradition, recorded as early as 500 B.C. in ancient Persian reliefs. Originally worn to symbolise status and age, earrings have evolved over time and across cultures to include a variety of distinctively modern styles, from ear jackets to drop chains.

Here are the most common earring styles to know:

STUDS—button-like, non-moving baubles that stay on the lobe of the ear

DROP—earrings that hang from the lobe for a dangling effect and most commonly have fish-hook posts

CRAWLERS—long and slightly curved earrings that climb up the earlobe towards the cartilage

HOOPS—circular earrings that connect through the lobe

CHANDELIERS—multi-tiered drop earrings that generally billow out as they hang and are often thought of as statement pieces

CARTILAGE—small earrings made specifically for cartilage piercings

FRONT-BACK—stud earrings that are decorative from both the front and back of the lobe

JACKET—earrings composed of a stud in the front and an ornamental piece that clips to the back and hugs the curve of the lobe

CUFF—wide, cuff-like earrings worn higher on the ear to hug the cartilage

In this chapter, see hairstyle inspiration to match your earrings, learn to mix and match studs for multiple piercings, follow our foolproof method for rocking massive ear cuffs in a non-abrasive way, and more.

How to Style
YOUR HAIR
with **EARRINGS**

THE STATEMENT
CHANDELIER ▶
- - - - - - - - - - - - - - - - - - -
Statement chandeliers
demand attention, so opt for a
simple up-do, like a ballerina
bun, to make these jewels the
focal point.

◀ THE BIG GOLD
HOOP
- - - - - - - - - - - - - - - - - - -
Big gold hoops require
zero fuss, so pair them
with a relaxed ponytail
for an effortless look.

THE MULTIPLE PIERCE ▶

Multiple piercings are all about subtlety, so why not go for a more complex hairdo like a side-swept French braid?

◀ THE MOONSTONE STUD

Moonstone studs may be understated in size, but their cosmic hues hold powers of their own. Make them shine with a simple pixie.

THE CRAWLER ▶

The half-cuff/half-stud crawler earring is an elegant way to bring attention to your ears. To keep things interesting, wear just a single stud on the other ear.

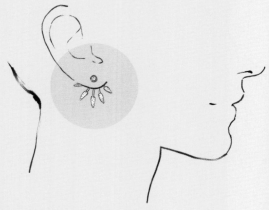

THE JACKET ▲

This two-for-one earring is a stud in the front with a jacket as an earring back. Keep it fresh by wearing it solo, or wear matching jacket earrings on both ears to edge up a more formal outfit.

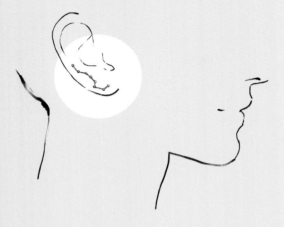

THE CUFF ▼

- -

Even if you don't have your ears pierced, you can still add a bit of shine with the ear cuff. Select a simple cuff in either gold or silver to slip around the cartilage of your ear, and remember to tuck your hair back!

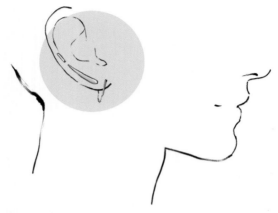

DAINTY AND DELICATE

1

Stick to one metal. Choose one type of metal—all of your earrings should be within the same family of materials. Yellow-gold or silver pieces work harmoniously together and create consistency.

2

Select a variety of styles. Whether you're into tiny hoops, chain drop earrings, long studs, or tiny gemstones, select a variety of earrings to experiment with. As long as the metals match, the earrings will look cohesive.

There are now plenty of chic earrings that are perfect for the multi-pierced ear. Check out the following ways to dress up all your multi-piercings.

- -

3
———

Go heavy to light or big to small. Wear the heaviest and/or drop pieces closest to your face, with the earrings lightening up as they move up the lobe. If you've got a drop earring and a heavier stud, always go with the drop earring first.

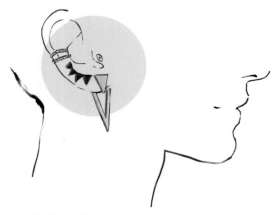

MATERIALLY MAXED OUT

1

Select your gemstones based on colour. Make your earring selections based on complementing jewel tones—it will help elevate the look. Stones such as ruby, emerald, diamond, and sapphire all look great with one another.

2

Choose an array of earring shapes and sizes. Go bold with each earring in varying shapes and sizes. Select geometric statement earrings, bold crawlers, and sparkly double cuffs—items that look wildly different from one another. As long as your gem colours complement one another, these bold earrings will work together.

3

Go heavy to light or big to small. Just like with delicate earrings, wear the heaviest and/ or drop pieces closest to your face, with the earrings lightening up as they move up the lobe. The piece that drops the farthest down should always be worn closest to the face.

AUTUMN ▶

Chunkier metal pieces that have
weight are best paired with a
neutrally coloured autumn hat to
keep the attention on your ears.

◀ WINTER

Keep your earrings simple with
plain studs that won't get caught
up in your heavier layers.

Earrings can be worn all year round, of course, but some styles work better based on season. Here are four styles to try when temperatures shift.

SPRING ▶

Radical large earrings with pretty gemstones are in sync with the blooming florals of springtime.

◀ SUMMER

Try a pair of tassels with an up-do and a light, breezy tank top for the summer months.

STYLE BY OCCASION

Bold, abstract drop earrings are a great staple in any jewellery collection, and it's easy to keep them in rotation all week.

WEEKEND

To keep the pair of accent earrings looking ultra casual, wear them with a sporty weekend outfit. Add a baseball cap to pull back messy hair—after all, you want these earrings to be on full display.

WEEKDAY

Nothing makes an office ensemble more interesting than a pair of earrings that shows off personality—plus, in a sea of button-downs and pencil skirts, baubles keep your look fresh.

How to Wear the FRONT + BACK EARRING

1

A single set of pearl studs is classic, but double the pearls with this earring back and you take this traditional jewellery look to the next level. The larger pearl is worn in the back so it peeps out from behind the lobe for a subtle but dramatic effect.

2

These intricately designed earrings, also known as the Balinese subeng, feature earring backs with twisted leaves that act as a continuation of the gold setting from the front.

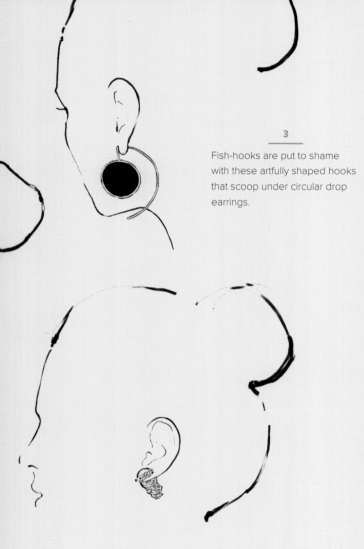

3

Fish-hooks are put to shame with these artfully shaped hooks that scoop under circular drop earrings.

THE BEST
EARRINGS
for Each Face Shape

	Oblong	*Oval*	*Round*	*Rectangular*
STUDS	√	√	√	√
ROUND	√	✕	✕	√
SQUARE	√	✕	✕	✕
TRIANGLE	√	√	√	√
EXTREME DROP	✕	√	√	✕
TOP-HEAVY	√	√	✕	√
BOTTOM-HEAVY	√	√	√	✕
CUFFS	√	√	√	√
CRAWLERS	√	√	√	√
JACKETS	√	√	√	√

Earrings can be worn by jewellery lovers of all face shapes, but it's helpful to have a quick cheat sheet on hand to find out what type of earrings are most flattering. The basic rule of thumb is to pay attention to proportion, so avoid earring types that are shaped too similarly to your face.

Inverted Triangle	Triangular	Square	Diamond	Heart
✓	✓	✗	✓	✓
✓	✗	✗	✓	✓
✓	✗	✗	✓	✓
✗	✗	✓	✗	✗
✗	✓	✓	✗	✗
✓	✗	✗	✓	✓
✓	✗	✓	✓	✓
✓	✓	✓	✓	✓
✓	✓	✓	✓	✓
✓	✓	✓	✓	✓

CHAPTER
SEVEN

EVERYTHING
ELSE

How to Wear the Rest

When it comes to personal adornment—
from hair jewels to decorative arm cuffs
—there are ornamental pieces that live
in a class all their own. Consider this
section a glimpse into a category full of
creative embellishments.

Here are a few pieces to know:

ARMLET—an arm band that looks like an oversized bracelet worn on the upper arm

RING-TO-WRIST BRACELET—chain jewellery worn over the hand and connected from the finger to the wrist

BODY CHAIN—delicate chain weaving that is worn across the front and back of the body

HAIR COMBS & HEADBANDS—decorative jewellery that is worn in the hair

Learn which outfits are best for rocking the body chain, see how jewelled pieces can be styled for hairdos, find out what to look for in an armlet, and more. See how these pieces break the rules when it comes to jewellery—and how you can incorporate these transcendent baubles into your own everyday style.

How to Wear
HAIR COMBS
+ HEADBANDS

─────

HEADBANDS ▶

- -

Once your up-do is pinned,
slip on a sparkly headband
to keep the front of your hair
in place. Ideal for a special
evening or a formal event,
headband jewellery is an
accessible take on the tiara.

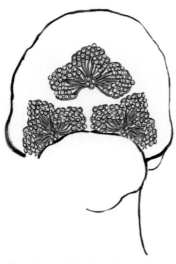

◀ HAIR COMB
CLUSTERS

- -

To amp up your hair from
the back, adorn a low bun
with a cluster of jewelled
hair combs. This creates a
stunning and unexpected
look, especially if you keep
your other jewellery on the
delicate side.

Sometimes the best pieces of jewellery are the ones that you incorporate into your hair — they provide a functional purpose by keeping an up-do in place, all while adding extravagance to the hairstyle.

SIDE HAIR COMBS ▷

For a romantic look, sweep your hair to the side and pin it with a large floral hair comb. Fitting for a garden party or a wedding ceremony, this off-centre comb elevates the simplest hairstyle into something photograph-worthy.

◁ REVERSE HEADBANDS

The reverse headband is perfect if you want to add a fancy twist to a loose hairstyle. Look for a Grecian-inspired laurel headband to accent a simple weekend jumper-and-jeans outfit.

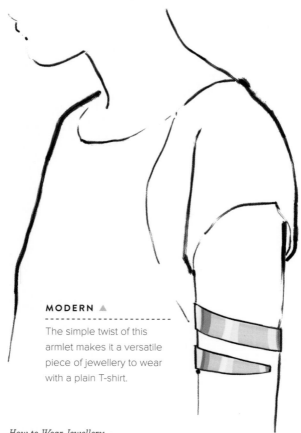

MODERN ▲

The simple twist of this armlet makes it a versatile piece of jewellery to wear with a plain T-shirt.

Flaunting an armlet is unexpected and daring. Check out these
three ways you can wear the armlet to your next outing.

ECLECTIC ▶

Select three thin armlets of
varying materials to create a
stack. Space them out so they
don't feel too tight, and stagger
the charms so they're not all in
a straight line.

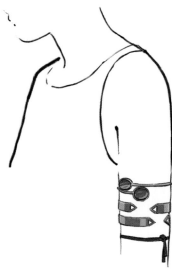

◀ VINTAGE

Consider the intricately detailed
vintage armlet a bona fide
statement piece. For a dramatic
effect, wear it for a formal event
with a Grecian-inspired one-
shouldered top.

How to Wear
RING-
TO-WRIST
BRACELETS

___

These hand-jewellery styles push the accessory envelope while still being simple to wear. Best worn without other rings or bracelets, ring-to-wrist bracelets are a gorgeous way to add a lot to an outfit with one piece of jewellery.

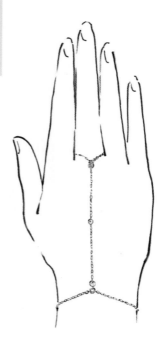

DELICATE

The most basic form of a ring-to-wrist bracelet is this subtle beauty. Perfect for a casual outfit, this piece is the accessory of choice when a naked hand needs a light embellishment.

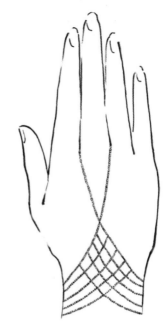

EMPHASIS ON RING
- -
This ring-to-wrist style focuses
on the ornately patterned ring.
A matching mid-hand pendant
draws the eye towards the wrist.

EMPHASIS ON WRIST
- -
A simple woven-chain loop worn
around the middle finger allows
for the bracelet elements of this
style to shine.

How to Wear
BODY
CHAINS

DRESSED UP

Wear a body chain that
is more dramatic for a
formal night out—look
for substantial hardware
details like a gold cross or
swooping chains that hang
past your hips. Pair with a
simple LBD to make the
gold stand out against the
dark fabric.

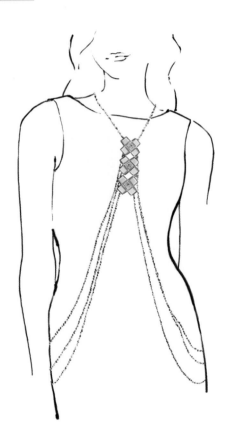

When looking for a body chain, choose one that doesn't fit too tightly around the body—you want to avoid snapping and breaking the chains—and that sits comfortably on your back and around your hips.

DRESSED DOWN

A body chain that you intend to wear in the daytime should be toned down. Select a form-fitting piece (with a tighter neckline or chains that hit above your hips) that you can wear over a long-sleeved top.

STORING + CARING

EARRINGS

If you have lots of fish-hook earrings, you may want to invest in an earring tree, a nifty contraption from which you can hang your drop earrings. To store stud earrings, grab a scrap piece of leather and poke holes in it with a thumbtack. Keep your earrings fastened to the leather for a quick and easy way to access your studs and keep them all in the same place.

NECKLACES

Depending on the types of necklaces you own, you may want to mount a set of hooks onto your wall that can hold your jewels. Hooks are great for both delicate and heavy statement pieces and they'll keep your necklaces from tangling. You can also look into necklace trees, which have designated branches from which your necklaces can neatly hang. For a more artful display, lay your necklaces out on slabs of marble or on books (vintage hardbacks look particularly sophisticated).

HOW TO DISPLAY & STORE YOUR JEWELLERY

While there is no wrong way to display your jewellery, there are strategic ways to store your earrings, bracelets, necklaces, and rings to keep your pieces as organised as possible. These tips will especially come in handy if you're the type to misplace pieces regularly.

BRACELETS

Bracelets are generally easier to store, especially if you have mostly cuffs and bangles. Non-adjustable bracelets are easy to stack onto a wooden or ceramic rod, or throw into a jewellery box, converted cigar box, or beautiful ceramic bowl. Delicate chain bracelets should be stored with care similar to your necklaces, preferably on hooks.

RINGS

Because of their size, rings look fantastic in a simple ceramic dish or a small bowl. There are also ceramic hand-shaped displays that you can invest in for next-level ring displaying.

PACK YOUR BAGS

Packing jewellery for travel is just as important as bringing the outfits themselves. The trick is to separate each piece to avoid tangles, which also helps you keep track of everything you've packed. Place each necklace, bracelet, and anything else that could get knotted into its own plastic bag and label it. All rings can go into another plastic bag. Secure all earrings to a piece of scrap leather (use a thumbtack to poke holes). Throw everything into a travel pouch and you're ready to go.

HOW TO CLEAN & POLISH YOUR JEWELLERY

Metals tarnish over time—you can't get around that. As long as brass, copper, gold, and silver are exposed to air and moisture, they will lose their lustre due to oxidation. But there are ways to get your beloved pieces back to their shiny new selves by using household products.

- For alloy metals such as brass, give those pieces a good scrub with ketchup for a quick polish.
- A mixture of lemon juice and salt is great for cleaning copper.
- For gold pieces that are not plated, use warm water and dish soap to give them a clean.
- A simple dab of toothpaste with a teeth-whitening component (that is not a gel) works particularly well on silver.

And, of course, if all else fails, you can always count on a jewellery-cleaning solution.

JEWELLERY RESOURCES

Aesa
http://www.aesajewelry.com
35 Crosby St.
New York, NY 10013

Bande des Quatres
http://bandedesquatres.com

Carbon & Hyde
http://carbonandhyde.com
801 S. Flower St., Suite 355
Los Angeles, CA 90017

Erica Weiner
http://ericaweiner.com
173 Elizabeth St.
New York, NY 10012

Erin Considine
http://erinconsidine.com

Highlow
http://www.highlowjewelry.com

In God We Trust NYC
http://ingodwetrustnyc.com
70 Greenpoint Ave.
Brooklyn, NY 11222

Lizzie Mandler Fine Jewelry
http://www.lizziemandler.com

Mociun
https://mociun.com
224 Wythe Ave.
Brooklyn, NY 11249

Pamela Love
http://www.pamelalovenyc.com
143 W. 29th St., Floor 4
New York, NY 10001

Selin Kent
http://www.selinkent.com

Tulola
http://www.shoptulola.com

Text by Jinnie Lee
Illustrations by Judith van den Hoek
Editor: Camaren Subhiyah
Production Manager: Anet Sirna-Bruder

Library of Congress Control Number: 2015949572

US ISBN: 978-1-4197-2019-2
UK ISBN: 978-1-4197-2257-8

Printed and bound in China
10 9 8 7 6 5 4 3 2 1

Abrams Image books are available at special discounts when purchased
in quantity for premiums and promotions as well as fundraising or
educational use. Special editions can also be created to specification.
For details, contact specialsales@abramsbooks.com or the
address below.

THE ART OF BOOKS SINCE 1949

115 West 18th Street
New York, NY 10011
www.abramsbooks.com